AESTHETICALLY AUDIBLY ME

Aesthetically Audibly Me

Tralyne Usry

Published by LuLu.com

Strong, James, *New Strong's Exhaustive Concordance of the Bible*, Nashville, TN: Thomas Nelson Publishers, 1990

ISBN 978-0-557-66058-2

Credits
Publishing Services LIFE More Publishing, Richmond VA
Copy Editor: Sandra Johnson

Photographer Keston Duke- Keston Duke (www.kestonduke.com)

Hairstylist Tishawna Pritchett – Hairstyles by Shawn- Shawn's Hair n More (www.shawns-stylez.com)

Cover Design: Apostle Lannice Collins, Richmond VA

Dedication

This dedication requires no contemplation!
It's to the Lord above that I dedicate this Love!
Without His love, mercy and grace,
I would not even be in this race!
For His Kingdom Purpose I strive!
Through His Blood, I'm alive.
To my Mommy and My Granny
From whom I am birthed
The portals to my safe passage to earth
Without your pushing, love, and guided support
My purpose, I would abort!
To My DADDY
May you rest in peace
I WILL accomplish the rest of your purpose
That God has left to me
Every dream you WERE to fulfill
I, your SEED, WILL MAKE IT REAL!
To Mi Tia, My Aunt, My Tauntee, My D,
Thank you for the daily investments in ME!
From birth till now
I will never understand how
You love me unconditionally!
Without you, I would not be

Mi Hermana, My Tezshjuana, My T.

You have believed in Me

To you I dedicate this work of art

For this accomplishment

You have been a great part!

To My Apostle, My Pastor, My Mah, My Friend

We ARE next of kin!

To you I dedicate

This stroke of the pen!

And to everyone else

Not mentioned by name

Because of your love and contributions

You, too, reside in MY HALL OF FAME!

Acknowledgements

It is with great enthusiasm and thanksgiving that I give praise to God for all that He has done. He has allowed this work of his hand to come forth, and I acknowledge Him as the TRUE AUTHOR. He inspires and guides my hand.

I would also like to thank God for my Mother Ms. Karen Dyers and the late Mr. Jimmy Usry who gave me life. Their lives have been a source of inspiration for me.

My sister, Tajuana Usry, has been a "rock" and a source of inspiration. Thank you for every seed sewn, and for believing in me! Because of you, I have been able to "Keep my head up, soldier!"

My Grandmother, Mrs. Ethel Louise Augusta Loving "Mae" Mitchell is my heartbeat. Her wisdom has been imparted and continues to help me make "life" decisions that will be passed on to my seed and my seed's seed. Granny, you already know, because I tell you every day; "Love ya, love ya, love ya!"

My "Tauntee", Ms. Donaval Mitchell has been present in every facet of my life, from the womb until now. For every tap shoe you spray painted, every graduation that you attended, and every sermon that you reminded me of, words cannot express my gratitude! You have done more than any aunt could ever have been expected to do. With my humblest gratitude, I salute you! You are the "Aunt of a Lifetime."

My spiritual father, Pastor Jesse Blake and his wife Theresa Blake, thank you for every seed sewn, every word of encouragement given, and your unconditional love!

To Apostle A.P. Scott, my spiritual mother, thank you for wrestling with me in prayer, and WORD to bring me through!

Thank you for leading me to the Father to find out that "The WORD is Life."

To My Apostle, my Ma, Apostle Ezreaonne Jackson, thanks for being a constant source of inspiration, a daily reminder that God is, and He can! You are an inspiration to millions and you don't even know it. I bless God for what He has deposited in me through you! Thank you for being my "John the Baptist," a forerunner for a lot of life's adventures.

Contents

Introduction

The purpose of this book is to reveal through visual images and audible sounds the character, the nature, and the person of God, thus the title *Aesthetically Audibly Me*. Aesthetic means of or pertaining to the sense of beauty and audibly means capable of being heard, thus the words that follow will both allow the partaker to see and hear the beauty of God and what HE has done for His people.

God has given us life and that life more abundantly. The ability to see Him is to be like Him (I John 3:2). When he appears to us in sound or in visual images, we attain a greater understanding of His person. To understand His person is to fall deeper in love with Him. The more in love we become, the easier obedience to Him becomes. Obedience to Him produces the abundance of life. God is very expressive. He speaks, He feels, He symbolizes. He expresses himself through song, through dance, through words, through deeds, through thoughts, through sentiments, through so many varied ways. God is not limited in His ability to express. This form of expression is poetry. It is simply an extension of His expression. The use of poetry by God is not new. Hebraic poetry is utilized throughout the Bible, from the Old Testament to the New Testament.

The structure of Hebraic poetry is not always easily identified because it does not depend on rhyme or the arrangement of sound but on the arrangement of thoughts, parallelism.

There are three basic forms of parallelism; synonymous, antiethical, and synthetic. In synonymous parallelism, the second line repeats the thought of the first. In Antiethical parallelism, the thought of the first line is emphasized by a contrasting statement in the next line. Synthetic parallelism is used when the second or succeeding lines build on the thought expressed in the first. Hebraic poetry often mixes these forms to express the heart of God.

There are three poetic books of the Old Testament these are Job, Psalms, and Ecclesiastes; however, poetry is used throughout the entire Bible. The book of Psalms contains the greatest number of poems. The word maschil is found in the title of some of the Psalms (KJV). Although the meaning of this word is not completely clear, some believe it indicates a special musical accompaniment. Maschil, in Hebrew, means instructive, i.e. a didactic poem. Didactic means morally instructive or intended to instruct. Thus the purpose of poetry inspired by God was accompanied by music and intended to instruct. Aesthetically Audibly Me was given by God for the same purpose. Every poem is intended to instruct you in the person and ways of righteousness. Enjoy every maschil!

Breath

I Timothy 4:2b says, “having their conscience seared with a hot iron”. Ephesians 4:19 says, “who being past feeling have given themselves over into lasciviousness, to work all uncleanness with greediness”.

Can’t you see the image of the surface of your conscience, with a hole piercing through to the very core?

This is exactly what happens as a result of sin, any sin, but especially the sin of fornication. To sear means to char, scorch, or burn the surface of with a hot instrument; A condition, as a scar, produced by searing. Sin makes an indelible print in our conscience, the print is not easily removed. In fact, it leaves a scar. That scar is a constant reminder of the sin itself and the missing of the mark. And sometimes, no matter how hard you try, or no matter how much you stay out of sin, there are still the horrible flashbacks and memories of what you have done. The bible states that the searing of the conscience keeps us in dead works. No matter how much we attempt to serve God, a seared conscience keeps us from being able to enter into all that He has promised.

When we come to the altar, be it in church or in private, we always come to God with this offering for our sins, our soiled conscience. God is not accepting this sacrifice anymore. The only sacrifice for sin that He acknowledges now and receives is the one that Jesus made. There is no mote sacrifice for sin; no other that God will accept; and our constant crying and whimpering about our past sins is not going to move Him. He wants truth. He wants the blood of Jesus. He wants His son.

This is the inspiration for this poem; my deliverance from a sin conscience. He whom the Son sets free is free indeed. There is life after sin and there is life without sin. Jesus purpose was to free us from the curse of the law and to gives us new life. The curse of the law was death (Gal 3:13, Romans 6:23. Man died because he broke the law, the law of God (Matthew 5:17). Jesus came to fulfill the law. The very law that the first man Adam could not keep, the 2nd man Adam fulfilled. Jesus, fully man, and fully God manifested the fulfillment of the law by not breaking the law. He was fully man. The Bible says that he was tempted like as man in every way yet He sinned not. SO it is possible to live as a man or woman in this earth and fulfill all of the laws of God. It is possible to live without sin and to live after sin. Jesus proved this because after He took on the sins of the world and died, He rose again. He did not sin himself but He took on everyone else's sin that we might have a chance at life.

Now you may be saying well that was Jesus and I am not Jesus- He was the Son of God. The Bible says that Jesus was born of God and a woman. When you accept Jesus into your heart, you are born again, which means that you are then born of a woman and born of God. I John3:2 says "beloved now are we the sons of God and it doth nor yet appear what we shall be but we know that when He shall appear we shall be like Him for we shall see Him as He is".

There is no way that anyone can say that being without sin is impossible. We are but flesh and we do not possess the ability to do that. The devil is a liar. We can do all things through Christ who strengthens us (Philippians 4:13), including defeating sin and the sin conscience!

Finally You

Burned, Seared
A hole completely through
Through your conscience mind
Through your eternally imprinted soul
Through the very you of you
And All For What?
A touch
A rub
A kiss here
And you know
THERE
Hopes built up high
Please brutha spare me the lie
The deceit of the trap
The misconception of the game
You were full of promises
Until You CAME
Now comes the instant replay
For your sins you must repay
Daily relenting
Daily repenting
Your sin is tormenting

How could you do it again?

How could you make the same mistake?

You thought the anointing oil would take

When Sunday in church, you admitted your mistake

But you see it's not a magic elixir

Olive oil is not a mind fixer

Your mind must be burned through anew

With the blood of Jesus

The work of the eternal spirit

Jesus' mind in you.

So come on boo

He went through

The same test and trials

Yet He sinned not

You can do it too

I, too feel relieved

My soul's been retrieved

FFFWW

Now Finally

I can breathe!

Notice Served

Men have a very powerful and awesome role to play in the lives of the women. Fathers of little girls, especially, have an intricate role to play. A girl's natural father gives her the picture of what her heavenly father is like. If the picture that she is seeing is not a good one, then the relationship with her heavenly father is strained, difficult, and sometimes seems impossible.

This poem was written at such a time in my life when I had been disappointed by every man that I came in contact with. My natural father was not there for me and had not been for most of my life. I was having a difficult time relating to my pastor and the man that I was dating had just disappointed me again. The only positive male figure that I had ever had was my grandfather, who by this time was getting sick. He was the only man that I knew that could take care of me and he now needed to be taken care of. This was not a pretty picture.

I was crying out to the Lord about this emptiness that I felt and this overwhelming anger that was developing. I was beginning to despise men, all men, any men. I did not trust them. I thought that they all had ulterior motives and that they only cared about themselves. I had to get this out of my heart because this was not the will of God. This poem became my therapy. After the poem was written, God ministered to me about a man a real man who cared about everyone else, excluding himself. He took on human flesh that all might be delivered.(John 3:16) This man loved me and would never leave me or even disappoint me. He promised to never leave me or forsake me (Hebrews 13:5).

Brutha Priest

My brutha's
Where are you?
Can I hear you holla loud?
Not from the jail cell
Or from the thug life
Or the wife beater crowd
But from the throne room
Your crowns wear
From the priesthood
Intercess there
For you wives
Your mothers
Your daughters
Please birth
And don't abort us

Imagine That

This poem was written as the answer to the contemplation of my spirit. When I am alone in my solitude with the Lord, I see all the things that have been placed in my spirit to accomplish. In the realm of the spirit, impossibilities cease. There are no limitations in the spirit (Philippians 4:13). The Bible says when I see Him I shall be like him for I shall see him as he is (I John 3:2-3). The ability to see Him is in the spirit. This is the same for the plans and goals that we have to accomplish. If we cannot see it, we cannot have it. Take a moment and think about impossibility. Think about something that seems insurmountable in the natural, but in the realm of the spirit in your imagination nothing is impossible. Our imagination is a gift from God that he has given that he may implant a plan and a dream. The imagination is the gateway to the spirit. When the imagination is ignited the spirit man is enlightened.

Imagination means the power of the mind to form a mental image or concept of something that is not real (tangible) or present. It also means the power of the mind that is used creatively. We were made in the image and the likeness of the creator. The Bible says that God is mindful of us. In the mind of God was the creation of man. Man, was first created in the mind of God and then God caused man to come to pass in the natural. The bible says as "A man thinketh in his heart so is he" (Proverbs 23:7). The word thinketh in the Hebrew means gatekeeper, or porter (Strong's 8176). Man is a quickening soul and a quickening spirit. By the very nature of his makeup whatever he allows into his mind it will be brought to life be it for good or bad. That is why the Bible says that we are to bring every thought unto the obedience of Christ (2 Corinthians 10:5). The Bible also says that we are to think on the pure things good things honest things (Philippians 4:8). Your imagination is a portal to the formation of actual worlds possibilities, things, every person who has ever been great had to ponder in their minds what they were about to do or partake of before they did it. The imagination is a gift from God. If you fill it with the word of God, which is the spirit of God, nothing shall be impossible to the people of God.

Four Corners

In the four corners of my room
Worlds are formed
Scripts are written, produced
Oscars are won
Grammy winning songs are sung
Global peace is attained
Addicts are reformed

In the four corners of my room
Christ is fully formed
The sinews of my vessel are immortally fortified
With the life ensuing blood of Christ
Jesus crucified

In the four corners of my room
How I long and I ache
I am in desperation
The walls are beginning to shake
I must have all of Christ

I must have him

Emphatically Speaking

I was trying to take a quick rest break before having to go to work. I was working the second shift and dreading it, so I would sometimes have to truly motivate myself to get up and go. This particular night I had a hard time. I was talking to the Lord and meditating on who He is and His ability to deal with my complaining, and then all of a sudden I heard a very emphatic MAN Please. You know how you say man please when somebody is asking you for something more and you have already given them the world? Like when your parents have given their children everything they think that they could possibly want and then all of a sudden the children ask for one more thing. This was the tone of the Man please. The concept of the poem immediately began to take shape and then the words began to flow. I was on the floor and the first piece of paper that I could get to was a telephone bill. This was not even a full sheet of paper. I began to write and was running out of space so I had to write around the perimeter of the paper and wherever I could find space. I wrote the poem in seven minutes with arrows point from one line to the next so that I would understand when I had to write it legibly.

God has grown weary of our complaining and our ceremonial behaviors. We look as if we have it together but that hidden man of the heart is always crying out for more. Isaiah 1:11-15 (NKJV) says "To what purpose is the multitude of your sacrifices to Me?" Says the Lord. I have had enough of your burnt offerings of rams and the fat of fed cattle. I do not delight in the blood of bulls or of lambs or goats. When you come to appear before me, who has required this from your hands to trample my courts? The New Moons, the Sabbaths, and the calling of assemblies — I cannot endure iniquity and the sacred meeting. Your New Moons and your appointed feasts My soul hates; They are a trouble to Me
I am weary of bearing them. When you spread out your hands, I will hide My eyes from you; Even though you make many prayers, I will not hear. Your hands are full of blood."

Man, Pleaz

I'm sick of y'all
Sick of y'all
Always talking
Saying I ain't walking
While the devil stalking
You with yo' big mouth
You still talking
Saying, I ain't Blessing
Steady stressing
Blaming Me
For the Regression
Of Your Procession
Man Please
I created the earth in 6 days
Didn't sit down 'til the 7th
For you I even left heaven
But I ain't walking
When the enemy came
Asking for you
Steady stalking
Forever gawking
Access denied

But you still talking
Running your lips
Flapping your trap
Talking that yang
Man pleaz
Shet yo' yap
Playing the same ole games
Sinning sipping tipping' slipping
But no ……………
You ain't to blame
I only died for you and you still insane
Crazy Loco Lunatic Deranged
Man pleaz
Are you ever gonna change?
You know
Transformation, salvation
The things my veins bled for you
What are you waiting for?
An invitation?
Man
Please

Rhythmic

I remember sitting at a CeCe Winans concert and being overwhelmed by the presence of the Lord. Ms. Winans was clearly at a new place in her worship and so was I. The anointing was so high and so pronounced that I did not know what to do with myself. Neither did Ms. Winans. In the middle of the worship service she was on her face before the Lord. This was wonderful to behold. In all of her efforts to take us into the throne room with the Lord, the people present were not getting it, some were but a vast majority were not.

The service was held inside a church that had a large open floor like a gymnasium. The pastor of the church was a young man excited for the Lord. There were vendors in this room and the people were allowed to shop while the worship service was going on, what an insult to the spirit of God. The presence was so thick and people's mouths were full of chicken wings and sausage dogs. I was so offended and I know that the Lord was appalled.

Even in the midst of all that I observed, my spirit man was being drawn to Him. I began to thank Him for allowing me to even experience His presence, His redemption, the work of His power. Then revelation began to break through me. Without Him having made me, I would not have experienced these benefits. He allowed me to exist in His creation. Wow what an honor and a privilege to be in the earth and on top of all that, to be saved and in the earth. Just being given existence in His beautiful creation is more than I deserve, but to be allowed to be saved and in that which He created, I was overwhelmed. That means that all that we partake of and all that we see belongs to us. We are heirs of God and joint heirs with Jesus Christ (Romans 8:17). We have inherited God. Our inheritance is literally God. Do you understand? We have not inherited millions of dollars, houses cars or land. We have inherited God. Those other things are just fringe benefits.

Seek ye first the kingdom, and HIS righteousness (Matthew 6:33). The kingdom is God. Why would it say it like that except the kingdom is a person? Go after God and the things that His son has inherited will be added unto you. We are joint heirs WITH Jesus, not of Jesus but with Jesus. Jesus was a gift not an inheritance. An inheritance only comes to children of a particular family. We were not of the family of God until Jesus came. His gift to us was himself, which was our adoption into the family. Now we can, and by right, have the inheritance that belongs to us. We have inherited God!

Existence

Given existence in His creation

Formed to be His expression

I've been forgiven

No longer searching for the blessing

Possessing the confession of my profession

Peaceful

This poem was written in two stages, which happened over a four-year period. The writing of the first part came when I was sitting quietly and allowing the Holy Spirit to speak to me. The conversation covered so many topic areas that I was being flooded with information and revelation. I could not contain all of it in my finite mind. Then I saw a vision of the way God reveals Himself to man. He is so large in His scope that He is not limited to any one method. So HE uses many things to accomplish one goal, revelation of Himself in us. He may use a dream, a vision, a word of prophecy, the birth of a child, whatever He chooses. And then with those things, He reveals another aspect of His character, His nature His person. But man determines at what pace and what amounts he will receive. We are made innately with choice and if we want to block something out, we will. We will tell God not now, in a minute. He is so patient that He simply waits until we say go. He is not forceful when it comes to revealing Himself. He simply waits on us. The opening of the door allows him to put together another piece of the puzzle. The image of who He is slowly, quickly, moderately, or sparingly is put together inside of us. He is a rewarder of those that diligently seek Him (Hebrews 11:6). Diligence determines the pace of the revelation of the image. Pick up the pace!

Although the revelation was great and life changing, I could not complete the poem because God desired that I go through some more things so that my understanding would be more mature. Then the second part could be written.

As we go through this journey, of receiving more of God, at the pace that we choose of course, things happen. Some of those things are very hard and harsh and make us doubt the presence of God. They make us doubt that they are an even greater revelation of His person. During those really hard times, we will find when we draw closer to God, those tough places and hard places were actually places that God led us to in order to make us who He has called us to be. Any place that God leads is a safe place.

Safe Place

In the deep recesses of my existence
Lingers the question
Why here God?
Why now?
Why not somewhere else?
Why not someone else?

My soul longs
With a steadfast hope
To answer, the unanswered
Trying to cope

Circumstance fashioned
To birth and unearth
A diamond in the rough
My, this does seem rough

Why did he abandon me?
Why didn't she see?
Why couldn't they hear?
Why did you create the deaf ear?

The longer I dwell

The more I understand

Pieces of the image
Innocently placed
Upon the hearts of man

Determined at his own pace
Each man receives
As much as He would allow
Opening and closing
The portals of his soul
Maintaining His existence at status quo

The gateway of his living blocked by his intellect
Or opened through a spirit check

If we allow
He will reveal
If we empty
He will fill

It is all up to us
He is a gentleman
He does not rush

Rush you to hear him

Rush you to feel Him

He gently nudges
And if our Heart budges
He trickles
He spills
He pours
Your willingness
Determines the score
Or the measure by which you meet
The Creator
The more is revealed
All of this was your plan
And…

You planned for me to hurt
You planned for me to search
You planned for me not to know
Through fire I was birthed
Safe Place

Harmony

God made man in his image and his likeness (Genesis 1:26), that means all of us. The enemy tried to make us believe, through racism, that God intended for there to be a separation of the races. There are also some who are of the mindset that God created a superior race. SO with this type of programming, the enemy implanted in the minds of people that we were not all created from the same fabric. God made us all shapes and sizes hues and ethnicities as his own expression. God is so vast in who He is that he cannot express himself in one thing or people. He is expressing everyday when he creates another child or when he allows the sun to shine. These are all countless expression of who He is. He is vast. He is wide. He is God. This poem was written to counteract racism. My tongue is the pen of a ready writer (Psalm 45:1). Ready to write and rewrite what will and must be in alignment with His Word. He has trained my hands for war and my fingers to do battle (Psalm 144).

BE

The content of the continent
Is a racial conglomerate?
Co mingling of fleshes
Hues, sizes, shapes
The enemy is irate
His plan was to separate
And dissipate
The plan of the most High potentate
But you see
Your skin don't intimidate me
I'm not offended by your ethnicity
Long or Short
Kinky hair or straight
Wide nose
Skinny lips
Not ever for me a source of debate
You look like my daddy
The beauty of his splendor
Take a glimpse into the mirror
And surrender
To the image
The original
See Him and be like Him

Free Him

And Just BE

Absence of Sound

This is the operation of sin in our lives. Sin is a silent killer, but the cry of it can deafen you for life. Sin will cause you not to be able to hear God, thus you are deaf. He that hath and ear let them hear what the spirit is saying to the church (Revelation 2:7).

Silent Operator

Deafening Silence
The loudest cry of sin
The travail of torment
Vivid from within
Heard in the spirit
Inaudible to the carnal
Inclined to keep silent
Relentless in Pursuits
Continuing in traditions
Bearing ridiculous fruits
Loss is gained
Connection between God and man cut in twain
With every law of God profaned
Trying to maintain
He can hear you screaming
Crying out for redeeming
Every outward act of sin
A cry from within
Longing for a King
Someone to take domain
Over the flesh that He already overcame
Defeating sin in the flesh

He already defeated this mess

Your cry was not heard by deaf ears

He was previously crucified

Even before the years

Dramatic Exposition

There was a burst in my spirit! I became overjoyed and excited and the only thing that came out of the experience was a loud overwhelming yell, OH MY GOD! God had sufficiently blown my mind for the 12 millionth time! I did not know what to say or do other than to yell Oh My God!

He Is

Is life worth living?
If, His voice I can't hear
The essence of my existence
The consistency of my living
For me there is not choice
The beat of my giving
You are it
You are Him
You are all
You are more
OH…………….. MY……………. GOD

Imperative

This poem was written in response to some things that were going on in my soul that were not lining up with the word. There were some things in my soul that I thought I had put under but they kept rising in my mind trying to get me to yield. No matter how far you think you have gone and no matter how much you think you have escaped the enemy tries to come back and tell you that you have not. This was the cry of my spirit speaking to my soul to conform. Ultimately Jesus is Lord and He will gain the victory.

From the Spirit to Soul w. Love

Why won't you conform?

Why won't you change?

Are you holding out for the flames?

You claim to be in the master's hands

Yielded to his command

Clay has never been mold retard

Why you trying to be so hard?

Every knee gone bow

Every tongue gone confess

Opening your own mouth

With willing surrender

Would be best

Don't make Him have to make you

Don't force his hand

Yield to the command

There ain't no escaping Him

You think you playing Him?

Either Get with Him

Or get burned

Will you ever learn?

Liquid Love

I was employed with a major Christian ministry as a prayer counselor. One of the requirements of every employee was that we attend two corporate worship assemblies, New Year's Eve, and Founders Day. On New Year's Day, 2002, I found myself in the presence of believers from all nationalities and faith levels, worshipping the Lord. The presence of God was so tangible and could be felt by anyone with a pulse. The praise and worship team sang like angels. The musicians played like they created the instruments themselves. The atmosphere was so perfect. My heart was free. My head was lifted. My countenance was bright, and my soul was in love all over again. I immediately started tried to think of ways that I could relive this moment. I envisioned women sitting around talking about a good date, or a good husband and the things they do. This poem was then birthed out of my conversation with my girlfriends, about the greatest lover of all times.

Have you ever?

Have you ever had anybody

To blow your mind

With like just one line?

Say something so sweet

That makes you feel complete

Have you ever had a brother say something so fierce?

That through all your defenses pierce?

You know the lines

That some men spout

Momentarily eliminating

And relieving any doubt

You know lines like

For you I'll cross an ocean

Without a notion

Or with you my sweet

I'm complete

You my universe

My stars

My world

You my girl!

Have you ever had a lover

A lover like no other?

So passionate

So sweet
Have you mesmerized
For a week?
    Have you ever known bliss
    From one single solitary kiss?
Have you ever?
Well I never
Not until
I met a lover
So real
    So deep
    So steep
    His words so sweet
One line
    I forgive
Translation
    You may live
Eternity is my hook
    The kiss of forever
    It is written
In the book
    He paralyzes my senses
    I need no defenses
I can't taste, touch smell, or see
The width of His adoration for me
    He permeates my existence

Made me a witness
A partaker of His glory
Yeah, this is my story
For me
He crossed eternity
The depth of sin
Was not too great
For you my love
I will wait
Wait on the cross
Until the work is done
Until with me
You'll be
Secured by the Son
And when it was finished
Full fellowship replenished
I can not be without you
I will not allow
Anything to separate
This is my solemn vow
Have you ever known a love like this?

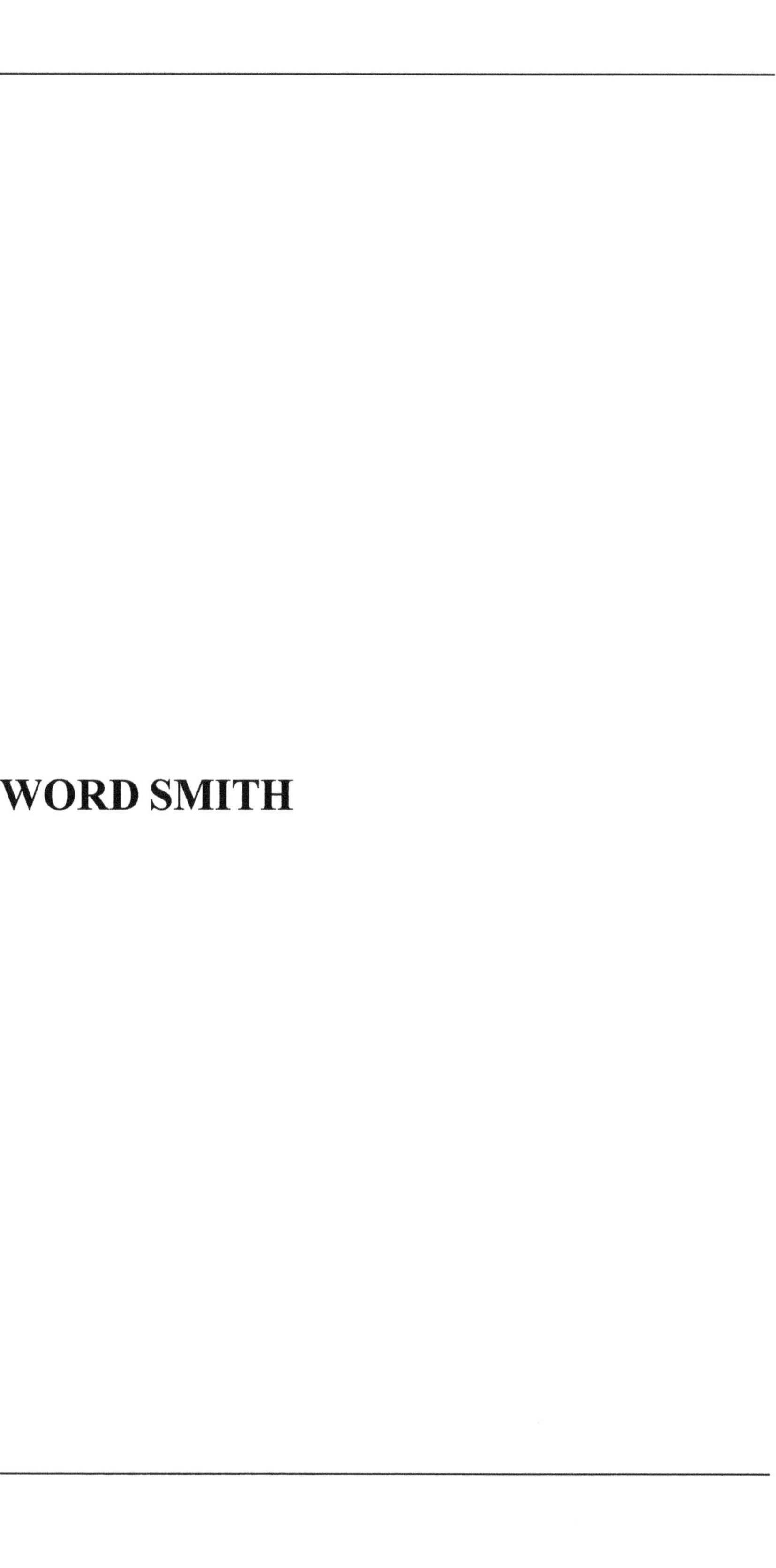

WORD SMITH

Spittin Emphasis

There's an emphasis
To every lyricists
Spittin this
Spewing life giving language
Or a knife
All of it is fluid
All of it lucid
Your decision?
Is it conducive?
You choose to absorb
Or refuse it
Check your emphasis
When you spittin'
You're responsible

Legally Speaking

It is illegal
How you flex
Walking with your dreams
Held high on your shoulders
In your eye it gleams
Just who do you think you are?
Just what do you presume to do ?
With your confidence
Your posture of possibility
Radiating and Lighting
Every Room
What are you thinking?
Just what is your shout about?
Do you really believe
That you bad like that?
Without a doubt
See legally speaking
Your heart should be leaking
Oozing fecal matter
From all the mess you gathered

Legally bound to the curse of the law
When you sinned

Your doom
The devil penned
See legally speaking
You belonged to him
You and your seed
Everything about you
Reflected his lead
But Jesus did the deed
Fulfilling the law
Erasing every flaw
All legality

Verbal Revolution

My phraseology is not an apology
But an admittance
That I am His
And He is Mine

Although politically incorrect
I must interject
JESUS IS THE KING

This is a Verbal Revolution
Spouting Creations Solution
Interrupting Satanic Pollution
Introducing................................

Verbal Revolution

Can you get with this?
'Cause you can't stop this

One **WORD** only
And the worlds were formed
One **WORD** only

Interrupting the norm

It took a **WORD** to create it

It took a **WORD** to devastate it

It will take a **WORD** to change

It will take a **WORD** to rearrange it

Speak a **WORD** only

Verbal Testimony

Let's start a revolution

Speak the solution

What's the **WORD?**

The **WORD** was made flesh and dwelt among us,and we beheld His Glory, the only begotten of the Father full of grace and truth. (John 1:14)

My phraseology is not an apology

But an admittance

That I am His

And He is Mine

It's pass time

To start a verbal revolution

Spoken Word Artist

Spoken word artist
Lyrical Giants
Prolific in their speech
Spouting mad science
Doing verbal stunts
Playing no games
Craftsmen of mind capture
Dazzling your brain

Artisans of the language
Expounding on the truth
Stunning
While they gunning
Spitting mad like vermouth

Breakin' Mic's
Setting the stage ablaze
Reverberating acoustics
Splitting P.A.'s

Essayists
Orators
Scribblers

Creators

Spoken word artists

Mad crazy originators

Not anything new

Or different from the rip

God

The master spoken word artist

Knocked chaos on its hip

Stepped out on the stage of nothingness

With an audience of none

Spoke worlds into existence

With a sentence

He placed the Sun

Formed Galaxies with Syntax

Formed planets with sentence structure

With a word

Spun Earth in its orbit

Can you absorb it?

And

As if that wasn't enough

Mind boggling stuff

He created you

Then said simply speak
And I will do

Whatever you ask the father
In my name
That will I give
From the words of your OWN mouth
You may live

So, Spoken word artist
Paint
Your canvas awaits

The canvas of life
Open your vocal box
Lyricize
Use the knife

The sword of the spirit
The word
Speak and activate
By engaging YOUR lips
You create
For you are a
SPOKEN WORD ARTIST

Without effort I write

Without effort I write
Scripting and penning
His mercy
His worth
His might
Without effort
I ignite liquid life
Spitting straight peace
Lucid love leaks
Dripping from my verbage
Trickling from my vocab
Spit spit spittin'
The light of life
Brings annihilation of strife
Without effort I write

The Kingdom

Power

Impact

Force

The kingdom,

Limitless!

"Ignant Wild"

"Ignant" Wild
You feeling me chile
Out of the wilderness
Hey, You hearing this
Blowing my mind
Yeah, my mind is now blown
By the massive expression
Of the invitation
To your throne
Can I come near you?
Can I come see?
Can I really be?
Made in the image of your deity?

"Ignant" Wild
You hearing me chile
Out of the wilderness
Hey, You feeling this
Blowing my cranium
My head is gone
Exploding my gray matter
Consuming My Dome

"Ignant" Wild
You feeling me chile
Out of the wilderness
Hey, Peep this
Preceded by a legacy
Of "ignant" wild folks
Eating locust and honey
Causing Pharisees to choke
(Matthew 3:4)
Crying Repent, Repent
For the kingdom is at hand
Roaming in the wilderness
John had to be a crazy man
(Matthew 3:2)

Isaiah
Naked and walking
Obeying the Word
To the sane
Absurd
(Isaiah 20:3)

Elijah calling for fire
On a heap of wetted logs
Just "ignant" enough
To defy natural laws
(I Kings 18:33)

Moses striking rocks
"Ignant" and wild
Securing mass exodus
Of the chosen child
(Exodus 17:6)

And then there's you
Just as "ignant" as they come
Wild enough to believe
In the risen Son
Letting this mind be in you
That mind that Jesus Knew
Equipment to obey the Father
This we will do
Holding up the blood stained banner
Declaring His reign
When all looks like chaos
You Praise
Insane in the membrane

Ignant wild
You feelin' me chile
Out of the wilderness
Hey, You ARE this
Just Ignant Wild!

Reality Check

What It Was

What it was
Is just what it is
No dress up
Or make up
Or cover up
Just time to fess up
Cause what it was
IS just what it is
Call it a weak moment
Call it what you wanna
Whatever you term it
It still Ain't gonna
Erase the fact
That what it was
Is just what it is
Yeah, you was underneath him
Call it lovin him
Or being there for Him
Supporting Him
Cause you care for Him
Or whatever
What it was

Is just what it is
Baby Girl don't be fooled
For him it wasn't about love
Respect
Or Devotion
The notion
Of swimming in your ocean
Was what set his attention in motion
Cause what it was
IS just what it is
You know you a queen
Accepting what you can get
Not demanding
Your own standard
Can I be candid?
What it was
Is just what it is
Baby Boy
Where your head at?
Trying to stay in the game
Trying to maintain
Fronting
Flexing
Clueless
Regressing
What it was

Is just what it is
Where you gone end up?
Where you heading?
Keep dipping and slipping
What you spreadin'?
Cause what it was
Is just what it is
It's been a fight from the beginning
The enemy of our flesh
Think he winning
Always suggesting the regressing
Never fessin' to your true blessin'
What it was
Is just what it is
Before the drama
Before the foundation
Ordained you
A prophet to the nations
What it was
Is just what it is
Knew you
Before you knew you
In eternity past
Before your great grandma
Was a twinkle
In your great great granddaddy eye

Before planets and stars loaded the sky
Even before God said let there be
In the mind of God
Was you and me
Cruising and Perusing
in Eternity
Cause what it was
Is Just what it is!

Are You Strong Enough?

Are you strong enough
To step in the place that I am in?
Can you follow me
In the spirit?
Will the revelation blend?
Can you through intercession
Come find me?
When deep in his arms
I long to be
You can't be in my space
If you can't keep pace
With insight lace
This heavenly place
Where were you
When within me
He placed the moon?
Within me
He hung the stars again
Where were you
When He said let there be light?
Within me He opens and ignites
Where were you Boaz?
Where are you now?

Are you existent Adam?

Honor your vow!

What Am I Supposed To Say?

You want me to act like everything is okay?
You want me to pretend that you ain't gone pay
When everyday with the enemy you lay?
Nah you see it don't work like that
The sewing is the reaping
The reaping is the sewing
Your own progress you slowing
You betta be knowing
What you getting yourself into
What you bargaining for
The gateway to life ain't an easy door
This walk will cost you
Please Know
This ain't no easy way to go
Limb, eye, leg or foot
All must go
If in your way
They begin to flow and show
You keep looking to me
like I can explain
Why your inferiority
You maintain
What am I supposed to say?
Believe in your heart?

And confess with your mouth
The Lord Jesus
Take God as your spouse?
But you've already done that
So what am I supposed to say?

Repent, Pray, Fast?
Change your ways?
Change your path?

But you've already done that
So what am I supposed to say?
Huh, Just what am I supposed to say?

Existence

The Man in the Mirror

Have you taken a look
At the man in the mirror
Have you presumed his reflection
By what you see?
The image looking back at you
Does it frighten
Consume
or
Are you delighted
By what you see
Are you peering through a glass dimly
(1 Corinthians 13:12)
Are you looking at the image through sin
Are you seeking through separation
From the Father's love
Again
What is reflecting in your heart
Is the truth your condition
Are you believing the lie
The contradiction
Beloved Now
We are now
Beloved Now

WE Are the Sons

The Sons of God

Not appearing yet what we shall be

But the promise of the when

You see him you shall be like Him

(1 John 3:2)

Eternally

Finally

The man in the mirror

Free

Against Logic

It's counter intuitive
        To trust
                Believe
                        And have faith
It's against logic
        To sit and patiently wait
                On a deity invisible
                        On a deity unseen
                                On the promise of the intangible
                        Washing and making clean
                That's why he bypasses the mind
        And goes straight for the heart to live
Until finally
                Surrender
                                Your gray matter gives

Subversive

Struggles of the Non Believer

A Journey In Finding God

Awareness of a need for something greater

Not a fascinator
Or a fabricator
But the real McCoy
So you ask your friends
Your neighbors
Your peeps
This whole religion thing gives me the creeps
Logic speaks
Now if the Bible really was written by man
Then who had a hand
A hand In placing the stars
The moon
The sun
Maybe evolution is where we begun?
Like apes we rock hard on the planet
Maybe this Jesus really is just a bandit
Abandoning His reality
Creating an illusion for yours
Creating lyrical, spiritual, religious Holy War
Bludgeoning Havoc on you Nors
Your brain cavity explores
It's chaotic

Searching

You know
I'm a flow it to ya
Like you really know it
Like it really is
Handle your biz
Here comes the pop quiz
If God is really real
Then how you really feel?
About rumors of war
Agony Blatantly Boars
A whole in your religious façade
Cause you can't answer this question called God
An enigma?
Please!
He's that times 20 million gees
Plus 10 of these
Why the babies crying?
Why the soldiers dying?
Why the president lying?
And terrorist still spying
Your pop quiz score
It ain't even a four
Cause you can't answer that

You can't even begin
To Pen
SO you research again
Nome Neo Rege Keyo
Searching from within
Meditating on this thing called sin
Asa lam a lakan
Wa alakam assalam
I'm still loss
Man come on

Who Turned Up The Volume?

Who turned up the volume?
My life is too loud
Screams of my soul
Overpowered by the crowd
The crowd of responsibilities
Pressures, Expectations
Words of well wishes
And comfort
No consolation
I'm crying inside
Masked by my smile
Wondering with desperation
Is it all really worthwhile?
In the midst of the saints
Fellowship laughter and peace
Soften and quiet the decibel
That will later again increase
Back Home Alone
In a puddle of tears
Searching for the same joy
Just experienced with my peers
Where did this come from?

Who touched the dial?
Who changed the station on my life?
Who made living so vile?
When I find Him
I will break His fingers
Each digit one by one
I have to come out of this
I have to overcome
This is not me
This in not who I am
This is not the life I ordered
This is a sham!

Deep Recesses

I just want to see Him

I just want to see Him
To behold Him
To look upon Him
Ooh when I see him
I'm gonna tell Him
How great this love affair was and is
I'm gonna tell Him
Oh how wonderful His flowers
His trees
His towers
His magnificent butterflies
His sand
Ooh when I see Him
When I see His hand
Caress his fingertips
Cherishing the piercing
With my lips
Yeah when I see Him
I'm gonna tell Him
Oh How much I love Him
When my words betray me
And become too few
I want him to know

Ooh ooh

I want him to know

I'm gonna tell Him

This experience has been deep

This experience has been

ooh when I see Him

Hey Now

There's a sweetness
To this completeness
I mean
He's been good
Not tropical smoothie good
But well of living water good
Cooling my thirsting
Satiating, Not wasting
My hunger
My longing
Baptizing
Surprising?
That's good, ain't it?

There's a boldness
To this wholeness
I mean
He in me
Man, that's fierce
Not Lincoln LS fierce
But authority in the earth fierce
Through the heavens pierce
Commanding and

Demanding

His Word to manifest

Every spoken Word

A conquest

That's fierce, ain't it!

There's a concern

That's unearned

I mean

He's attentive

He bottles every tear

Simultaneously annihilating every fear

Hears every groan and moan

Returns harvest for every seed I've ever sown

All because of His love

That's attentive

The Eternal Chapter

It's Just Like Water

Traces of humility
Subtle hints of His grace
Tiny drops of his love
Radiating from your face
Cooling my thirsting
Satisfying my
Longing
The image of
Him
Prolonging…
It's Just Like Water

Queendom

Hey kingdom folk
This is not a joke
The king's domain
Birthed through a woman
Dominion proclaimed
Queendom

You have no idea of your wealth
No idea of your stealth
Can you not recognize?
Your very existence
The enemy
The slew foot
The devil
Despised

Did you think it was a game
When after you
The woman he came?
He could have come after Adam
But He understood
Adam only planted the seed
Birthing a nation He never could

He didn't possess a womb
A birthing canal
Receive the instruction
Heed this maschil

My sister
My love
My daughter
My queen
To the kingdom of God
You are everything

The woman
The church
The birther of the Man-child
Archer
Warrior
You can't be mild
You must step out of the shadows
Quit hiding
Come out of obscurity
In the kingdom abiding

Queen
Your queendom awaits

Your scepter is righteousness
Your diadem is peace
Your ashes are beauty
Your crown is grace

For in you
The fullness of eternity dwells
Wear it and Wear it Well

And The Next

I have no pleasure in the death of them that dieth (Ezekiel 18:32)
That enemy lieth
Saying death is a welcome friend
Come again?
My word says
I dieth no more
So if I live in you
I've evened the score
There are no more penalties to be paid
Foundation for your living already laid
Wages for sin is always death
Acceptance of me
Secures the next breath
And the next
And the next
And the next……….

The Poet

Tralyne DeShae Usry was born on May 11, 1976 in Augusta, GA. She is the daughter of Mrs. Karen M. Dyers and the late Mr. Jimmy L. Usry. She is the granddaughter of Mrs. Ethel A. Mitchell and the late Mr. Joseph W. Mitchell. She is also the surrogate daughter of her aunt Ms. Donaval J. Mitchell who has been instrumental in every facet of her life from conception to now and is in close relationship with her maternal grandmother, Mother Mitchell.

Tralyne attended undergraduate school at Paine College in Augusta, where she graduated with at B.A. in Communication, with an emphasis in print journalism. She studied at Regent University in Virginia Beach, VA, Directing for Film and Television. She is studying to receive a Master's in Education from Ashford University, Iowa.

She was taught in the admonition of God at the one of the oldest churches in Augusta, Georgia, Thankful Baptist Church. However, she did not accept Jesus Christ as her personal savior until she was 18 years old on March 3, 1995 at 2:30 a.m. This happened during a shut-in under the leadership of Prophetess Juanita Bynum-Weeks of Waycross, GA. She was further nurtured and brought into sonship (maturity) at the Word Is Life Church where she received her Minister's License in 1997 under the leadership of Apostle Aline and Pastor Martrice Scott.

Upon moving to Virginia Beach, to attend Regent University, God begin to funnel a new anointing to write and perform poetry. Since then, she has written a collection of poetry and spoken word pieces. She was also fortunate to participate in a contest to be named Hampton Roads Rising Gospel Artist. After winning the contest, she appeared on the Bobby Jones New Artist Showcase which aired on the WORD Network September 18, 2004.

She completed her first missionary journey to Jamaica where she served on the praise and worship team, as an altar attendant, and an intercessor.

She is now a member of the Greater Touch of Compassion Ministries, Richmond VA under the leadership of

Apostle Ezreaonne Jackson where she very excitedly serves as a Board Member, a Youth Director, Member of the Voices of Compassion Praise and Worship team, Director and Choreographer for Expressed Glory (liturgical dance team).

Minister Tralyne has been blessed with the opportunity to minister on various denominational and non-denominational platforms. Her passion for God and the desire to see others experience His love is phenomenal and promises to change your life.

She serves as the five-fold ministry gift of a teacher. The mantle upon her shoulders is to manifest life by defeating death in every area. God has blessed her with a great passion and enthusiasm for sharing with the world God's word concerning, "the last enemy to be defeated is death." Do you want to live? Hear this teacher!

www.ingramcontent.com/pod-product-compliance
Ingram Content Group UK Ltd.
Pitfield, Milton Keynes, MK11 3LW, UK
UKHW041926190726
13854UKWH00003B/1477